Super 3 Day Detox
Soup & Smoothie Plan

How To Cleanse Your Body With
Vegetable Smoothies,
Slow Cooker Soups & Fresh Fruits

✍

Geoff & Vicky Wells

Reluctant Vegetarians
Volume 2

Cover Artwork & Design by
Old Geezer Designs

Published in the United States by
Authentic English Recipes
an imprint of
DataIsland Software LLC,
Hollywood, Florida

https://ebooks.geezerguides.com

ISBN-13: 978-1494732974

ISBN-10: 1494732971

BONUS ~ Claim Your Free Book

Thank you for buying this book! As a bonus we would like to give you another one absolutely free - No Strings Attached

You can choose any of the books in our catalog as your bonus. Just use this link or scan the QR code below -

https://fun.geezerguides.com/freebook

Table of Contents

THE 3-DAY DETOX PROGRAM

DETOX RECIPES

BREAKFAST SMOOTHIES

Lunch Smoothies

Dinner Slow Cooker Soups

Appendix

DISCLAIMER

This publication is intended to provide helpful and informative material. It is not intended to diagnose, treat, cure, or prevent any health problem or condition, nor is intended to replace the advice of a physician. No action should be taken solely on the contents of this book. Always consult your physician or qualified health-care professional on any matters regarding your health and before adopting any suggestions in this book or drawing inferences from it.

The author and publisher specifically disclaim all responsibility for any liability, loss or risk, personal or otherwise, which is incurred as a consequence, directly or indirectly, from the use or application of any contents of this book.

Any and all product names referenced within this book are the trademarks of their respective owners. None of these owners have sponsored, authorized, endorsed, or approved this book.

Always read all information provided by the manufacturers' product labels before using their products. The author and publisher are not responsible for claims made by manufacturers.

Having said that, Vicky recently had an encounter with a medical professional who questioned her vegetarianism and whether or not she was getting sufficient calcium in her diet. Vicky told her that she ate lots of calcium-rich vegetables, such as kale and broccoli. The doctor insisted that those vegetables contained iron, but not calcium. Vicky begged to differ but the doctor was adamant. Vicky decided to double check her facts after that encounter. Kale and broccoli do, indeed, contain calcium and you can check out those and other foods at the USDA National Nutrient Database

http://ndb.nal.usda.gov/ndb/search/list - a searchable database.

We advise you to do your own research as well, particularly on how dairy milk can actually leech calcium from your bones. Cow's milk is great - for baby cows!

Medical doctors get little or no nutrition training. So, if your doctor tries to steer you away from a vegetarian or vegan diet, maybe it's time to look for another doctor. Fortunately, our family doctor is very much into fitness and has applauded our decision and congratulated us on our new lifestyle, diet and weight loss.

Introduction

Thank you for purchasing our book. We hope you will find it interesting and a helpful guide to a simple detox program.

This is the second book in our Reluctant Vegetarian series. The first book, A Guide to Juicing, Raw Foods and Superfoods, was a result of our decision to switch to a vegetarian lifestyle and our desire to share what we learned and experienced.

We felt that the next step in our journey was to develop a detox program that worked for us. This book is a result of our research and our own experience using exactly what we include here.

Amazingly enough, even though we thought it would be difficult, we found that becoming, and remaining, vegetarians was much easier than we had ever anticipated.

We found the same with this 3-day detox - it was easier than expected and we reaped the benefits from it. And you can too.

CANDID INTERVIEW WITH THE AUTHORS

As you're already vegetarians, what made you decide to detox as well?

GEOFF

When we first switched to a plant-based diet we both lost quite a bit of weight right off the bat, but then, after a while, that slowed down, so the detox was just a way to try and kick start the weight loss again.

Vicky: Since going vegetarian we did lose a significant amount of weight, which was very encouraging. But then we went for several weeks without actually losing anything - not gaining anything. But we decided to try a detox, a short detox - just three days - to help jump start the system again.

Why did you use smoothies and soups instead of juicing?

GEOFF

I want to lose weight but I don't want to be hungry while I'm doing it. So, the idea of using soups and smoothies, which have a lot more bulk than juice, just appealed to me.

VICKY

We decided to use smoothies and soups for this detox because juicing -I don't like the idea with juicing that you take out the fiber. I like the fiber to stay in what I'm eating, particularly during a detox to help clean things out. And, the idea of the smoothies, we kept all the fiber in. The idea of the soups was to be able to actually have something hot for the evening meal and something that you could actually chew. And, that seemed to work very well for us.

Did the three day detox work for both of you?

GEOFF

We didn't have our blood analyzed but I felt better and I lost another 5 pounds. So, yes, it worked.

VICKY

Yes, the detox worked for me as well. Over the three days I was actually able to lose four pounds, which I thought was pretty good. So, yes, the detox did work for us.

Did you find the detox difficult to follow?

GEOFF

I don't have a lot of will power when it comes to food. The first couple of days were not too bad but I have to admit by the end of the third day I was getting a little hungry. I was glad when it was over but, no, not really difficult.

VICKY

I wouldn't say it was difficult to follow just different from our normal pattern of eating. I was glad it was a short detox because, again, it's a departure from the way we normally eat. It was okay for a few days and some of the recipes were actually pretty good. No, I didn't find it difficult.

Did either of you lose weight over the three days?

GEOFF

As I said, over the course of the three days I lost almost 5 pounds and then that kick started the system so over the next few weeks I lost even more. Of course we've slowed down to almost nothing now so it's probably time to do it again.

VICKY

Yes, we both did lose weight. As mentioned earlier, I lost four pounds, Geoff lost five. So, yes, we both lost weight during detox.

Did either of you experience any side effects from detoxing?

GEOFF

No, nothing you'd consider a side effect, unless, of course, you count an irrational craving for a grilled cheese sandwich.

VICKY

I wouldn't say I experienced any side effects from the detox other than - well, the losing weight was good side effect. But, I was trotting off to the bathroom a little more often than usual and I'm sure that helped with eliminating whatever toxins we were getting rid of.

What Are the Benefits of a Detox Program?

First and foremost a detox program helps your body to eliminate accumulated toxins and waste. We are all exposed to toxins everyday through the air we breathe, the foods we eat and any medications or drugs (prescribed or otherwise) we take.

It is entirely possible that you're carrying around a lot of excess fecal matter (yes, poop!) that has not been effectively eliminated from your colon - particularly if you're a meat-eater. The human digestive system is much more similar to that of an herbivore than a carnivore. The human digestive system is much longer than that of a carnivore. A carnivore digestive system is much more acidic, breaking down food much faster, and smoother, allowing for a quicker elimination of waste without the need for fiber. Our digestive system takes a considerably longer time and requires fiber to help things move along. The slower the process the more time for waste to accumulate and putrefy in your body.

Once this excess waste is eliminated you should experience increased energy levels, not to mention some weight loss, too.

In addition, removing old waste and toxins from your body helps to strengthen your immune system and will even improve the health of your skin and hair.

WHAT ARE THE POTENTIAL SIDE EFFECTS OF A DETOX PROGRAM?

While very few people experience any side effects at all, it's still best to be aware of some of the potential side effects of a detox program.

You should always consult your personal physician before starting any detox program, particularly if you are being treated for any chronic diseases.

If you experience any of the these symptoms, some of them may be the result of sugar or caffeine withdrawal and should only be mild. However, if you find that any side effects are particularly difficult, then stop your detox program and see your doctor.

Here are some possible side effects:

- Headaches
- Fatigue
- Increased Thirst (remember to stay hydrated!)
- Increased Urination
- Increased Energy
- Moodiness
- Sore Muscles
- Insomnia
- Weakness
- Restlessness
- Diarrhea
- Lack of Appetite

Listen to your body.

Tips for Choosing Your Fruits, Vegetables and Herbs

Why Organic is Best

There are many good reasons to choose organic produce over conventionally grown. The first and foremost, of course, is the lack of chemical fertilizers and pesticides. Naturally, avoiding chemical fertilizers and pesticides is good for you.

However, did you know that that's not the only benefit of purchasing organically grown food? Here's a few other advantages to think about:

- organic produce is much less likely to be GMO (Genetically Modified Organism)
- organic produce is much less likely to be grown as a mono-culture (grown as a single crop on a massive scale)
- organic methods of growing actually improve the soil quality. That means you get more nutrition from the produce that is grown this way while protecting and nurturing the soil. Conventionally grown, mono-culture produce depletes the soil. That's why they need to apply so many chemical fertilizers, pesticides and herbicides. That also means that you get less nutrition and fewer micro-nutrients from conventionally grown food.

Bottom line - if you have access to, and can afford, organically grown food, then that's the way to go. If you're not able to afford all organically grown produce, then at least try to avoid buying the conventionally grown items on the most-contaminated list and opt for organic instead. Also, be sure to use the Fruit and Vegetable Wash on anything that is conventionally grown.

Why Raw is Best

Needless to say, eating raw, organic produce is best. But why?

Heating foods over a certain temperature (about 118°F or 48°C) destroys a lot of the nutrients found in raw foods. It can also destroy the enzymes in the food that help you to absorb the nutrients.

But raw food is also good for the environment. There's little to no packaging and what packaging there is (rinds, peels, etc.) can be composted. That's good for the soil.

By eating raw produce you'll also notice that you're a lot more regular thanks to all the fiber.

These are just a few of the benefits of raw foods. Another one is that you'll just plain feel better. So eat raw when you can.

Note: We like to keep things raw when we can but not everyone (us included) likes everything to be raw all the time. That's one of the reasons we've included slow cooker dinners for this detox plan. Yes, you'll lose some of the nutrients by cooking the food, but it also makes for a tasty dinner.

All the smoothies in this detox plan use raw foods and any dessert you choose to have should consist of raw fruits.

THE FOODS WE USED AND WHY

You'll be amazed at the marvelous properties that most fresh produce and herbs have. One thing you'll want to watch for, though, is to make sure, wherever possible, that you choose organic produce, particularly for the foods that are on the "most contaminated list".

We have marked each item that is on the most contaminated list as well as those that are on the least contaminated list.

In any case, it's always best to go with organic produce if you can.

APPLES

We've all heard the saying - "An apple a day keeps the doctor away." Well, it's good advice.

We all know that apples are good for us, but did you know just how much they contribute to detoxing your body?

Apples give you fiber, vitamins, minerals, phytochemicals, flavonoids and terpenoids - all of which help the detox process. The flavonoid phlorizin is thought to stimulate bile production, which helps the liver get rid of toxins.

Apples also contain pectin which helps eliminate metals and food additives.

Be sure to buy organic apples whenever possible because apples are, unfortunately, on the most contaminated list.

APPLE CIDER VINEGAR WITH "THE MOTHER"

Be sure to purchase unfiltered, unpasteurized organic apple cider vinegar with "the mother". This is apple cider vinegar at its purest form without the goodness being filtered away or destroyed by the heat of the pasteurization process.

The many other benefits of genuine apple cider vinegar make it a great addition to any detox plan. Studies have shown that it can increase metabolism while generating energy and reducing hunger. It also plays a role in detoxing the liver.

Other benefits include easing nighttime leg cramps, lowering cholesterol and controlling blood sugar levels.

ASPARAGUS

Asparagus has an amazing list of benefits and supports much more than detoxification, although it is especially good at supporting liver detox.

It is a natural anti-inflammatory and antioxidant while also having anti-cancer benefits.

This vegetable has a unique way of supporting digestion. It contains a substance called inulin which passes through, undigested, to the large intestines. This then feeds the friendly bacteria that aid in proper nutrient absorption.

Asparagus is included in the least contaminated produce list, which is good news. Even still, it's always a good idea to buy organic when you can.

Avocado

Even though avocados are relatively high in fat, the health benefits far outweigh the extra calories.

Avocados have both soluble and insoluble fiber which helps with detox and weight loss. They also contain oleic acid which activates the part of the brain that tells you you're full.

Because consuming avocados helps to slow digestion it also helps to regulate blood sugar, a great way to prevent diabetes.

Avocados are on the least contaminated produce list, but it's still always a good idea to buy organically grown produce whenever possible.

Bananas

Bananas contain lots of phytonutrients and antioxidants along with being convenient and tasty. They're good all by themselves and also add a sweet creaminess to smoothies, not to mention what a wonderful "ice cream" they can make by putting frozen bananas (and other frozen fruit) in a food processor.

But it doesn't stop there, oh no!

Being a rich source of potassium they help to restore your electrolyte balance, provide energy, lower the risk of stroke and the fibre helps promote cardiovascular health.

Bananas are also a natural antacid which can help to protect the stomach from ulcers while stimulating the cells that make up the acid-protective lining of your stomach.

Bananas contain tryptophan which helps to regulate mood, sleep, memory and learning by aiding the production of serotonin. In addition, they are a rich source of fructooligosaccharide that nourishes the helpful bacteria in the digestive tract. This provides better digestion and processing of vitamins and minerals.

Bananas are also on the least contaminated list but, and we know we're starting to sound like a broken record, buying organic is always the best choice.

BASIL

Herbs and spices are a great way to jazz up just about any food, but their benefits don't end there.

Basil, often referred to as "sweet basil" is a relatively common herb that pairs well with tomato-based cuisine and is used extensively in Italian dishes.

However, basil packs quite a healthy punch, too. It contains the antioxidant beta carotene that protects cells from free radicals and helps to lower bad cholesterol. It's a good source of magnesium and that helps to maintain good cardiovascular health.

It also helps alleviate constipation, making it a good addition to any detox program.

BEETS

It's a good idea to include beets in any detox program you undertake and in your regular, day-to-day diet, too.

Beets support a detox regimen by supporting good gallbladder and liver health.

They contain Vitamins B3, B6, C, beta carotene, iron, magnesium, zinc and calcium - all of which are essential for elimination of toxins from the body. Their high fiber content also aids with the ultimate elimination of the toxins through bowel movements.

Don't be alarmed! You may think there is blood in your stool after eating beets. I know we've had to remind ourselves many times, when we see what looks like blood, that we have had beets in our diet. The reddish stools should go away after a day or two.

Use fresh beets if you can, rather than the canned ones.

BEET GREENS

When purchasing fresh beets, look for the ones that still have their greens attached because the greens are not only edible, but very good for you, too.

Beet greens are rich in Vitamin K which aids in blood clotting, and is now being studied for the possibility that it might fight Alzheimer's and osteoporosis.

The amount of Vitamin A found in beet greens is impressive and this vitamin helps to protect vision and fight the onset of night blindness. It also stimulates the development of antibodies and white blood cells and, therefore, may play a part in cancer prevention.

The beta carotene, a well known antioxidant, in beet greens also fights free radicals that can lead to premature aging.

BLUEBERRIES

Blueberries are a genuine detox powerhouse. Packed with fiber and Vitamin C, while being low in calories, they also deliver a significant antioxidant effect.

Their blue color comes from pigments called anthocyanins that help protect our cells from free radical damage and guard against heart disease, allergies, diabetes and even some forms of cancer.

The fact that blueberries are tasty makes it easy to add them to your regular diet, too, not just while detoxing.

BOK CHOY

Bok Choy is a cruciferous vegetable just like cabbage, broccoli, kale and Brussels sprouts. And, it shares a lot of the same benefits from this group of vegetables.

Most people don't realize it but it is a good, easily absorbed source of calcium. With plenty of fiber and beta-carotene, it also aids in efficient elimination of waste and helps reduce signs of aging by reducing free radicals.

In addition to this, it helps detoxify the liver, too.

BROCCOLI

Broccoli, part of the cruciferous family of vegetables, has lots of benefits aside from being a good part of a detox regimen.

If you've reduced or eliminated your intake of dairy products, as we have, then broccoli is a great way to get both calcium and Vitamin K that are important for bone health and the prevention of osteoporosis. As a matter of fact, dairy products can actually leach calcium from your bones, rather than strengthening them. So broccoli, and other plant-based sources of calcium, are a much better choice.

Of course, the soluble fiber found in broccoli helps in detox as it increases the speed that foods travel through your intestines. That's also a great way to reduce the risk of colon cancer.

All of the cruciferous vegetables contain powerful antioxidants that fight free radicals and slow aging. Another good reason to choose broccoli is because it is also on the least contaminated produce list.

So - eat your broccoli!

CABBAGE

Cabbage is one of the most readily available and reasonably priced of all the detox foods and still has some amazing benefits.

The fiber in this cruciferous vegetable not only helps to lower cholesterol, it also aid in digestion and quicker elimination through the bowels.

Different types of cabbage have different, yet effective, benefits. So be sure to try several different kinds such as red cabbage and savoy aside from the standard type.

Cabbage has also made it to the least contaminated produce list. Good news.

CARROTS

Most people think of carrots as being good for eyesight, and they're right, but it doesn't stop there.

Aside from anti-oxidants that control free radical and slow cell aging, carrots contain Vitamin A which helps the liver flush out toxins.

The amount of fiber in carrots helps clean out the colon and prevent constipation.

In addition, carrots also contain lots of Vitamin D, E, B6, K and more.

CELERY

It goes without saying, but we're going to say it anyway - celery is a great source of fiber and an excellent source of Vitamin C.

It also offers a good source of folic acid, potassium, calcium and Vitamins B1, B2 and B6.

Studies have shown that coumarins, the phytochemical compounds found in celery, are effective in cancer prevention. Studies also show that celery may lower cholesterol by aiding in detoxification.

Be sure to buy organic celery whenever possible because celery is, unfortunately, on the most contaminated list.

Citrus Fruit (Lemons, Limes, Oranges, Grapefruits)

All citrus fruits are packed with Vitamin C, an amazing immune system supporting nutrient, but did you know that they are naturally antiseptic and antimicrobial?

They are an essential part of any detox plan because they support proper liver function, help improve the absorption of minerals, cleanse the blood, aid in digestion and, of course, encourage the elimination of fat.

Lemons, limes and grapefruits contain a phytonutrient, limonoids. It's a powerful antioxidant and aids in the production of enzymes that help detoxify the liver and also help to clear toxins from the mouth, skin, lungs and colon.

Coconut Water

It's time to throw away those energy drinks and have coconut water instead. It's a natural electrolyte and an isotonic drink that increases the body's metabolism.

Coconut water is so versatile that, in a pinch, it can be used as a short-term intravenous fluid for rehydration, according to the American Journal of Emergency Medicine.

It's packed full of vitamins, minerals and other nutrients but has a lot less sugar and sodium than those sports drinks. It also makes you feel full faster and reduces food cravings.

Because it helps keep you hydrated, while also supplying a lot of nutrients, it's a great choice when detoxing.

CUCUMBER

We've found that most people like cucumbers, we certainly do. As it turns out, they are not only great for a detox regimen, but great any other time, too.

Being 95 percent water, cucumbers not only rehydrate the body but help flush out toxins while supplying lots of vitamins, too.

Make sure that when you eat them you leave the skin on. The skin will give you about 10 percent of your recommended daily allowance of Vitamin C.

The fiber in cucumbers is not only effective in removing toxins from the digestive system, it is often seen as a remedy for chronic constipation.

Other Vitamins and minerals you'll find in cucumbers are: Vitamins A, B1, B6, C and D, folate, calcium, magnesium and potassium.

DILL

Dill has long been a favorite herb and shows up in all kinds of recipes, but particularly in pickles.

It boasts impressive benefits. As a good source of plant-based calcium it can help to strengthen bones and prevent bone loss. It's natural anti-bacterial properties help to fight off infections.

It also fights free radicals and aids in digestion while helping to reduce bad breath and acid reflux.

Its essential oils can also have a calming effect on the body and help produce more restful sleep.

GARLIC

So, we already know that garlic is good for keeping vampires away, right? Okay, just kidding.

Even so, it's a great tool in your detox arsenal. It has been shown that crushed garlic can kill many different types of bacteria, including salmonella.

When it's heated it produces a compound that reduces serum cholesterol. It also contains Vitamins A, B and C which can help rid the body of toxins and help to fight certain carcinogens.

The sulfur compounds found in garlic help to regulate blood sugar and detoxify the liver.

On top of all this, garlic tastes great and adds a special flavor to lots of dishes.

GRAPES

Grapes are natural detoxifiers. During detox, grapes help with elimination of toxins through the bowels as they contain organic acid, sugar and cellulose (an insoluble fiber) that work as a natural laxative.

The two flavonoids found in grapes, resveratrol and quercetin, help to filter toxins from the blood and also neutralize free radicals.

In addition, grapes greatly reduce the acidity of uric acid and help remove uric acid from the body, reducing stress on the kidneys.

Red grapes, in particular, have powerful antibacterial and antiviral properties that can protect the body from infections.

Make an effort to buy organic, locally grown grapes whenever possible because imported grapes are on the most contaminated list.

HONEYDEW MELONS

Honeydew melons are not only an excellent source of vitamin C, they are also a good source for potassium, copper and several B vitamins such as thiamine, niacin, B6 and pantothenic acid.

Their high water content, in combination with the potassium, is helpful in maintaining normal blood pressure levels and keeping you hydrated, as well.

They also provide nutrients that are essential for healthy skin.

On top of all this, honeydew melons are also low in calories, so what's not to like?

KALE

Kale is fast becoming one of the most frequently touted super foods and for very good reasons. It's health benefits are truly amazing and you'll want to be sure to not only have this as part of your detox regimen, but use it on a regular basis the rest of the time, too.

It is very nutritious and supplies the body with antioxidant and anti-inflammatory properties. It has high levels of beta carotene, Vitamins C and K, lutein and calcium.

Kale produces sulforaphane when it is chopped or chewed. This helps the liver to produce enzymes that detox cancer causing chemicals.

Kale is also an excellent source of the flavonoid maempferol which has been shown to reduce the risk of ovarian cancer.

Kale also has carotenoid that help protect your eyes from ultraviolet damage and chlorophyll that helps detox the liver and the body. Chlorophyll helps to remove heavy metals, pesticides and herbicides.

We could go on and on about the benefits of kale and we encourage you to research this impressive vegetable, too.

Organically grown kale has a much higher concentration of phytonutrients than the conventionally grown kind. So be sure to get organic if you can - or grown your own.

NECTARINES/PEACHES

In any of the smoothie recipes, feel free to use either nectarines or peaches where one or the other is called for.

Peaches are actually native to China and are considered a sacred symbol of longevity.

Aside from being low in calories they also contain an amazing array of phytonutrients, vitamin, minerals and fiber. The phytonutrients and the Vitamin A (in the form of beta carotene) both help protect against certain cancers. The Vitamin C helps to boost the immune system and protect against heart disease.

The iron and potassium they contain help to maintain proper cell function and the balance of electrolytes, while the lutein promotes eye health and guards against blindness.

These fruits are also on the most contaminated list, so be sure to buy organic when possible.

ONIONS

Onions are a tasty staple that most of us use on a regular basis. That's a good thing because they also help to keep us healthy.

The phytochemical in onions assist the body in effectively using Vitamin C, while it also helps to reduce inflammation and heal infections.

They also fight free radicals and helps to regulate blood sugar.

Raw onion aids in the production of good cholesterol which is essential in keeping your heart healthy.

Although it's always best to buy organic, it's good to know that onions are on the least contaminated produce list.

PARSLEY

Often used as a garnish, parsley is so much more than that.

Parsley is great for detox as it contains Vitamin C, Vitamin K, chlorophyll, beta carotene and folate. It also guards against liver dysfunction caused by insulin resistance, a growing problem in our modern times.

Did you know that parsley is also a great breath freshener? Just chew on a piece of raw parsley for instantly fresh breath. So don't overlook that "garnish" on your dish.

PEARS

Pears are packed full of good-for-you benefits. Their high fiber content can not only keep you regular, but help prevent colon cancer, as well.

In addition, they boast lots of vitamins such as A, B2, B3, B6, C and K. And the minerals they contain include calcium, magnesium, potassium, copper and manganese.

In other words, they help protect your immune system and may help to prevent certain types of cancers, too.

Try to buy organic pears whenever possible because pears are, unfortunately, on the most contaminated list.

PLUMS

Most of us are already aware of the benefits of dried plums (prunes) but the fresh fruit also has many, many benefits.

Just like in blueberries, reddish-purple plums also contain the pigment anthocyanins which protects us against free radicals. A single plum contains about 113mg of potassium which helps control high blood pressure and reduces the risk of stroke.

Plums are also low on the glycemic index so they can help control blood sugar levels and lower the risk of type 2 Diabetes.

RED RADISHES

I'll bet that most of you have grown radishes in your garden from time to time. They are easy to grow and what's more organic than growing them yourself? So, no excuse not to add organic radishes to your diet.

As far as detox goes, radishes contain many potent nutrients to help the process along. They help to cleanse the liver, digestive system and the blood.

It's amazing what's packed into this little powerhouses. They contain vitamins C, B6, E, A, and K, antioxidants, fiber and several minerals including zinc, phosphorous, copper, calcium, magnesium, potassium, iron and manganese. Add to that the carbohydrates and protein that help keep you energized.

You'll never look at radishes the same way again.

ROSEMARY

We love to use various spices in our foods and they do so much more than just add flavor.

Tasty Rosemary is anti-bacterial, anti-fungal, anti-viral and aids in the detoxification of the liver. In addition, it also helps clean out the colon while increasing blood circulation to the brain. Feeling a bit foggy? Add some Rosemary to your food or homemade vitamin water.

RUTABAGA

Rutabaga, often referred to as turnips or yellow turnips, are actually a cross between a turnip and a cabbage. Originally developed in Russia, they now grow throughout North America.

Rutabagas are high in Vitamin C which aids in digestion and is associated with a reduced risk of colorectal cancer.

They are also a good source of zinc which supports the immune system and proper metabolism. In addition they supply a lot of dietary fiber which reduces constipation and increases the speed of elimination. A great way to detox the colon.

SPINACH

Popeye aside, spinach is actually a good-for-you superfood. It's high in nutrients, low in calories and can be used in all sorts of recipes or just on its own.

At only 7 calories for an entire cup, it's packed with Vitamins A, C, E and K, as well as niacin, zinc, folate, calcium and potassium.

It can aid digestion and ease constipation, flushing toxins out of the colon.

It has powerful antioxidant and anti-inflammatory properties that can help fight off disease. On top of that, it's great for the skin, too, relieving dry, itchy skin while promoting a clearer complexion.

Be sure to get organic spinach if at all possible. Why? Check out the most contaminated list of produce grown with the use of chemical herbicides, pesticides and fertilizers.

STRAWBERRIES

Aside from being just plain delicious, strawberries have significant benefits.

There are high levels of Vitamin C packed into these water-rich (almost 90%) fruits, as well as Vitamins A, C, E and K. In addition, you'll find folic acid and iron.

Natural purification by consuming foods like strawberries assists in the renewal and function of the liver and kidneys.

Some experts suggest that the consumption of strawberries contributes to heart health as they have anti-inflammatory properties.

Be sure to purchase organic strawberries whenever possible as the non-organic ones have been sprayed with all manner of toxins. Strawberries are one of the food on the most contaminated list.

TOMATOES

Lycopene, the red pigment found in tomatoes and other vegetables, is an amazingly powerful antioxidant. Tomatoes help detoxify the liver and the intestines.

Anti-aging experts maintain that lycopene can help people retain better health as they age because of reduced damage from free radicals.

While raw tomatoes are considered a good source of lycopene, cooking them provides a more concentrated supply because heating them breaks down the cell walls.

It good to note that heating tomatoes does not affect its health-promoting qualities.

TURMERIC

Turmeric is often used in Indian and Chinese cooking and has many health benefits. It's also the spice the gives prepared mustard its bright yellow color.

It is known to be an anti-inflammatory, anti-viral, anti-bacterial, anti-fungal, anti-carcinogen and antioxidant. Wow!

Turmeric is a natural liver detoxifier and painkiller helping to ease headaches, muscle aches and joint pain. In Chinese medicine it is also used as a treatment for depression.

Be sure to add this tasty, versatile spice to your collection and use it often.

What the Colors of Foods Mean

Having a rainbow of colors on your plate probably means you're getting a balanced and nutritious diet. Here's why you should vary the colors of the fruits and vegetables you eat.

Red Fruits and Vegetables

Red indicates that the produce may contain such nutrients as lycopene, ellagic acid, Quercetin, Herperidin and more. Not only can they help to reduce the risk of prostate cancer, they can also help to lower blood pressure and LDL cholesterol. In addition to that they can reduce free radicals and promote healthy joint tissue for arthritis sufferers.

Orange and Yellow Fruits and Vegetables

These colors indicate the presence of beta carotene, flavonoids, lycopene, potassium and Vitamin C. Such nutrients can help lower LDL cholesterol, control blood pressure and reduce free radicals. Along with magnesium and calcium, these nutrients can also help to build strong bones.

Green Fruits and Vegetables

Many green fruits and vegetables contain chlorophyll, fiber, lutein, calcium, folate, Vitamin C, calcium and beta carotene. These nutrients can help aid proper digestion, reduce free radicals, stimulate the immune system and support eye health.

BLUE AND PURPLE FRUITS AND VEGETABLES

Fruits and vegetables with these colors frequently contain lutein, resveratrol, Vitamin C, fiber, flavonoids, ellagic acid and quercetin. These nutrients help support eye health, lower LDL cholesterol and protect the digestive tract from carcinogens. On top of that, they support a healthy immune system and improve the absorption of calcium and other minerals.

WHITE FRUITS AND VEGETABLES

Although white may seem like the most boring color, fruits and vegetables that are white frequently contain a host of nutrients including beta-glucans, EGCG, SDG and lignans. These nutrients give the immune system a potent boost. They also help to activate natural "killer" B and T cells, thereby reducing the risk of hormone-related cancers by helping to balance hormone levels.

Most and Least Contaminated Fruits and Vegetables

According to the Environmental Working Group, these are the 12 most contaminated fruits and vegetables, followed by a list of the 12 least contaminated. So, if you're on a budget and can only afford so much organic produce, try to buy organic versions of the items on the most-contaminated list.

12 Most Contaminated Foods

- Peaches
- Apples
- Sweet Bell Peppers
- Celery
- Nectarines
- Strawberries
- Cherries
- Pears
- Grapes (Imported)
- Spinach
- Lettuce
- Potatoes

12 Least Contaminated Foods

- Onions
- Avocado
- Sweet Corn (Frozen)
- Pineapples
- Mango
- Asparagus
- Sweet Peas (Frozen)
- Kiwi Fruit
- Bananas
- Cabbage
- Broccoli
- Papaya

What NOT to Consume While Detoxing

It should go without saying, but while you're doing this detox, just follow the plan. That means you'll ONLY be consuming the smoothies, slow cooker soups, vitamin water and fruit desserts that are on the 3-day plan, along with lots of water to help keep you hydrated.

Don't consume any alcohol during this time (again, this should go without saying - but we're saying it anyway).

Also, no coffee, no tea (except for the green tea), no sugar, no bread, no meat - you get the idea.

Stay Hydrated While Detoxing

Staying Hydrated While Detoxing

What is Vitamin Water?

Vitamin water is becoming very popular right now. Basically, it's just water flavored with fruit and/or vegetables and/or herbs. But don't buy the commercial brands because it's really easy to make your own. We have included some vitamin water recipes in the recipe section of this book.

Water - Bottled or Not?

Contrary to popular belief, bottled water is no healthier (and may even be LESS healthy) than municipal tap water. Actually, most bottled water, if it doesn't cross state lines, isn't even regulated by the FDA. However, municipal water supplies are subject to strict regulations and are regularly tested for bacteria and toxic chemicals.

Besides just the purity of the water, bottled water creates an enormous plastic bottle waste problem, not to mention the current findings of plastic bottles, left in hot cars, outgassing toxic chemicals into the water.

Why risk it?

If you want to check out the safety of water in your municipality in the United States, visit the Environmental Working Group's National Tap Water Database http://www.ewg.org/tap-water/

Also, you can always filter your tap water, if it makes you feel better, using commercially available water filtering systems.

Green Tea

Green tea is not just a drink to replace your coffee while you detox, it's also good for you. It does contain some caffeine, about 15 to 40 milligrams per cup), so you won't be going "cold turkey" off caffeine. Green tea is not only a powerful antioxidant, it can also help protect the liver and may even help to guard against heart disease and some cancers.

Plan Ahead

Before starting a detox program, even one that only lasts three days, it's best to plan ahead and prepare.

Commitment

The first thing to do is to commit to a three-day period for the detox. Make sure you can complete the program, start to finish. You don't want to have to stop a day or two in and lose all the benefits that you've worked so hard for.

Mind-set

We've always found that the proper mind-set will see you through. You need to be doing this for yourself, for your own health and not for any other reason. Certainly not because someone else wants you to do this, for whatever reason. You need to know that by doing this you are being good to yourself, not depriving yourself.

Preparation

Preparation is key to a successful 3-day detox regimen. That means making sure you have all the fruits, veggies, herbs you need as well as having the kitchen utensil that you will need, like a quality blender for the smoothies and a slow cooker for the soups.

We also like to prepare and freeze a lot of the ingredients for our smoothies ahead of time and in the correct, pre-measured amounts. That just makes it so much easier, especially first thing in the morning.

Keep A Record

Keeping a record of your detox can be as simple or elaborate as you like. Here are a few suggestions for what to include in your record:

1. Weigh in on the morning of your first day before you've had anything to eat or drink. This gives you your starting point baseline weight. While this detox regimen is not about weight loss but rather about detoxing your system, odds are you'll also lose a little weight in the bargain. If you don't worry about it. You've still done something really good for your body.

2. Each day, record everything you eat and drink and when. So a diary or journal that has each day broken up into hours is a good thing. You can keep the journal either manually or on your computer. Also, record how you're feeling and any other things you're noticing such as increased urination (remember to keep hydrated!), bowel movements and things like that.

3. Weigh in again on the morning of the fourth day, after you've completed your detox, and record your weight again. And do something nice for yourself on that day to celebrate successfully completing your detox!

Some people may feel compelled to weigh themselves each day during detox. We don't recommend it, but it's not going to hurt anything. We just prefer waiting for the surprise at the end.

FOOD SAFETY

Always be sure to clean and handle your foods properly. Even if you purchase all organic produce, wash it well before using it. For non-organically produced fruits and vegetables, be sure to use the Fruit and Vegetable wash. You'll find the recipe for the Fruit and Vegetable wash in the recipes section.

USE UP YOUR SMOOTHIES

If you don't use all of your smoothie right after making it, be sure to store any leftovers in the refrigerator. If you don't use the leftovers within 24 hours, then throw it out.

LEFTOVER DETOX SOUP

Leftover slow cooker soups will keep longer in the refrigerator. They will also freeze well, too. So if you don't use up all the soups, freeze them for later use, even when you're not detoxing, because they are really tasty.

HOW OFTEN SHOULD YOU DETOX?

It is our suggestion that, once you have completed your first 3-day detox, you should commit to one detox day each month. Set aside a day when you can be sure to be able to complete a full day of detox and, of course, be sure to plan ahead and prepare everything you need, just as you have for your 3-day detox.

You can choose any of the breakfast and lunch detox smoothies and any of the detox soups. So, if you have particular favorites, then just use those.

THE 3-DAY DETOX PROGRAM

Now it's time to get started on your 3-day detox. Make sure that you've committed to the full three days and that you've got everything you need to successfully complete your detox.

As mentioned earlier, it's a good idea to prepare a lot of your food items in advance to save time each day.

Day 1 Menu

Start each day with a cup of green tea (no sweetener of any kind)

Breakfast

Detox Breakfast Smoothie #1

Lunch

Detox Lunch Smoothie #1

Dinner

Detox Slow Cooker Soup #1

Dessert

Fresh fruit of your choice - raw

Vitamin water and/or regular water and/or green tea throughout the day

Day 2 Menu

Start each day with a cup of green tea (no sweetener of any kind)

BREAKFAST

Detox Breakfast Smoothie #2

LUNCH

Detox Lunch Smoothie #2

DINNER

Detox Slow Cooker Soup #2

DESSERT

Fresh fruit of your choice - raw

Vitamin water and/or regular water and/or green tea throughout the day

Day 3 Menu

Start each day with a cup of green tea (no sweetener of any kind)

BREAKFAST

Detox Breakfast Smoothie #3

LUNCH

Detox Lunch Smoothie #3

DINNER

Detox Slow Cooker Soup #3

DESSERT

Fresh fruit of your choice - raw

Vitamin water and/or regular water and/or green tea throughout the day

Detox Recipes

Here is the list of the recipes we used for our 3-day detox. We certainly enjoyed developing the recipes based on the what fruits and vegetables were not only good for detox but just plain good for us, as well.

They worked well for us and we hope they do for you, too.

BREAKFAST SMOOTHIES

These delicious fruit smoothies will get your day off to a great start

Detox Breakfast Smoothie #1

Ingredients:

½ large honey dew melon, remove seeds and rind
1 cup (200g) strawberries, sliced
1 cup (100g) baby spinach, packed
1 cup (100g) blueberries
1 medium plum, pitted and chopped
1 banana

Directions:

1. Place all ingredients in a blender and blend until smooth. Add water to thin, if required.

   Note: *some of the fruit may be frozen (e.g. strawberries, blueberries, banana), if desired.*

Servings: 2

Detox Breakfast Smoothie #2

Ingredients:

2 plums, pitted and chopped
2 bananas, frozen
2 oranges, peeled
2 cups (475 mL) coconut water
1 cup (100g) spinach, packed

Directions:

1. Place all ingredients in blender and blend until smooth.

Servings: 2

Detox Breakfast Smoothie #3

Ingredients:

½ large honeydew melon, remove seeds and rind
2 medium nectarine, pitted and chopped
1 medium plum, pitted and chopped
1 cup (100g) blueberries
2 banana, frozen
2 cups (200g) baby spinach, packed
10 seedless grapes

Directions:

1. Place all ingredients in blender, except the water, and blend until smooth.

   Note: *Add water to thin, if necessary.*

Servings: 2

LUNCH SMOOTHIES

Detox Lunch Smoothie #1

Ingredients:

1 large cooked beet, sliced
2 medium carrots, chunked
2 medium red radish, quartered
2 cloves garlic
1 medium apple, seeded and cored
2 medium tomatoes, chopped
2 stalks celery, chopped
2 cups (200g) kale, packed, stems removed
½ teaspoon (2.5 mL) turmeric
3 cups (700 mL) water
1 tablespoon (15 mL) fresh dill, or 1 tsp dry
2 tablespoons (30 mL) apple cider vinegar, preferably unfiltered and with "the Mother"
5 drops tabasco sauce, optional

Directions:

1. Combine all ingredients in a blender and blend until smooth.

   Note: *We found that the addition of a little Tabasco and slightly warming this smoothie brought out the flavors the best.*

Servings: 2

Detox Lunch Smoothie #2

Ingredients:

2 medium pears, chopped
½ medium avocado, chopped
½ medium cucumber, chopped
1 large tomato, chopped
1 cup (100g) beet greens, packed, stems included
2 stalks celery, chopped
½ inch ginger, piece, minced
2 cups (475 mL) coconut water
2 tablespoons (30 mL) lime juice, freshly squeezed

Directions:

1. Place all ingredients in a blender and blend until smooth.

Servings: 2

Detox Lunch Smoothie #3

Ingredients:

3 large tomatoes, chopped
2 medium apples, seeded and cored
2 medium carrots, chopped
½ medium beet, cooked
1 stalk celery, chopped
2 shakes tabasco sauce
2 cups (475 mL) water

Directions:

1. Place all ingredients in a blender and blend until smooth.

Servings: 2

DINNER SLOW COOKER SOUPS

Detox Slow Cooker Soup #1

Ingredients:

1 large yellow onion, large dice
2 large carrots, chopped
½ head red cabbage, cut in chunks
1 cup (170g) bok choy, chopped
4 red radishes, quartered
2 large tomatoes, diced
6 sprigs parsley, chopped
2 stalks celery, chopped
1 medium summer squash, chopped
2 cups (475 mL) vegetable broth, or water
3 cloves garlic, minced
½ inch fresh ginger, peeled and minced
1 tablespoon (15 mL) soy sauce
1½ teaspoons (7.5 mL) dried rosemary
½ pound (225g) asparagus, cut in 2 inch pieces

Directions:

1. Place all of the ingredients in a slow cooker, with the exception of the asparagus, and cook on low for 8 hours.

2. 30 minutes before the soup is done, add the asparagus and turn the slow cooker back up to high.

3. When asparagus is soft, serve immediately.

Servings: 2

DETOX SLOW COOKER SOUP #2

INGREDIENTS:

½ large yellow onion, chopped

½ large red onion, chopped

3 cloves garlic, minced

3 cups (450g) carrots, chopped

2 stalks celery, chopped

½ large rutabaga, peeled and chopped

2 cups (475 mL) vegetable broth

1 tablespoon (15 mL) soy sauce

28 ounces (820 mL) canned tomatoes, crushed

1 teaspoon (5 mL) turmeric

1 tablespoon (15 mL) italian seasoning

½ lemon, thinly sliced, including peel

2 cups (200g) kale, thinly sliced, stems removed

DIRECTIONS:

1. Combine all ingredients in slow cooker with the exception of the kale.

2. Set slow cooker to low and cook for 8 hours.

3. 20 minutes before the soup is done, turn the slow cooker to high and add the kale.

SERVINGS: 2

Detox Slow Cooker Soup #3

Ingredients:

½ large yellow onion, chopped
½ large red onion, chopped
2 cups (350g) broccoli, cut in bite-size pieces
2 cups (220g) cauliflower, cut in bite-size pieces
2 cups (300g) carrots, chopped
4 red radishes, quartered
2 stalks celery, chopped
½ large rutabaga, peeled and chopped
2 cups (240 mL) vegetable broth, or water
1 key lime, thinly sliced including skin
1 inch fresh ginger, peeled and chopped
2 cloves garlic, chopped
1 teaspoon (5 mL) turmeric
1½ teaspoons (7.5 mL) rosemary
1½ teaspoons (7.5 mL) basil
1 cup (100g) baby spinach, packed
1 cup (100g) kale, thinly sliced, stalks removed

Directions:

1. Combine all ingredients in slow cooker with the exception of the the spinach and the kale.

2. Set slow cooker to low and cook for 8 hours.

3. 20 minutes before the soup is done, turn the slow cooker to high and add the spinach and the kale.

Servings: 2

Detox Vitamin Water

Ingredients:

 1 pink grapefruit, sliced
 1 orange, sliced
 2 key limes, quartered
 10 green seedless grapes, halved
 4 inches cucumber, sliced
 5 mint leaves, bruised
 2 tablespoons (30 mL) apple cider vinegar, with "The Mother"
 12 cups (2.8 L) water

Directions:

1. Combine all ingredients in a large jug and refrigerate for at least 8 hours before using.

   Note: *With all this citrus and the addition of apple cider vinegar, this is not only a detox vitamin water, it is also a fat burner.*

Servings: 12 - 8 ounce (240 mL) servings

Bonus Recipe

Fruit and Vegetable Wash

Here's a quick, easy and versatile fruit and vegetable wash.

1. Fill a large bowl with equal parts of cold water and white vinegar.

2. Soak less delicate fruits and vegetables, such as apples, carrots, etc. for 10-15 minutes. Then rinse well and pat dry.

3. Soak more delicate fruits and vegetables, such as berries and lettuce, etc. for 1-2 minutes. Then rinse well and pat or spin dry.

   Note: *The vinegar helps to dissolve any waxes, remove any pesticides and kill any bacteria. Don't worry about any "vinegary" taste. As long as you rinse everything well after washing the food, there will be no residual taste.*

Conclusion

While we have done an extensive amount of research before developing and testing this detox program, it is always wise to take the time to do your own research. There is a lot of information out there and it is a good idea to make sure that any information you encounter and decide to use if from a reputable source.

All results mentioned are our own personal results. All recipes in the book have been developed and tested by Geoff and Vicky Wells.

APPENDIX

That's it you've come to the end - now go back and make something.

When you have made a few of the recipes please go back to where you purchased and leave a review. There are millions of books available and the most important asset an independent author can have is reviews from satisfied readers.

We hope you enjoyed this book and find the information valuable.

Don't forget to choose your free book using the link at the beginning. There really are no strings, we just want to make sure you get good value.

In the next couple of pages you will learn how you can get a free membership to our Instant Pot video site and also how you can get another one of our books (your choice) absolutely free.

And please don't forget to leave a review!

Thank you,

Geoff & Vicky Wells

INSTANT POT RECIPES

The Instant Pot has now found an important place in our kitchen. We use it every day and have converted many of our favorite recipes to work in the Instant Pot.

We use this new appliance so much we decided to create a membership web site devoted to Instant Pot recipes. If you own an Instant Pot or are thinking of buying one we invite you to join us.

https://instantpotvideorecipes.com

As one of our loyal readers you get a free membership to this site as a bonus for buying this book. All you do is visit the secret claim page to get your 100% discount coupon code.

https://fun.geezerguides.com/freemembership

About The Authors

Geoff Wells and his wife, Vicky, were not the healthiest people when they first got married. They lived hectic lifestyles and opted, on many nights, to settle for something that was quick and easy, rather than something healthy and nutritious. When health issues, and weight gain, started to manifest, they decided that a more healthy solution had to be found.

They started to do their research and came upon the idea of juicing. It provided a healthy alternative to their current food choices and they found that juicing took very little time. So their weight loss adventure began but they also wanted to be sure that they were keeping everything in balance. After all, it wasn't just about weight loss but healthy eating, too. After additional research they found out about raw foods and Superfoods.

After seeing the positive results from modifying their diet they made the decision to share what they had learned with all who were interested. Geoff and Vicky believe they have found the key to living a healthy lifestyle and are proud to share what they know thus far. It is simple to follow and they have provided a large number of recipes to make switching to this type of lifestyle even easier.

Update

Geoff and Vicky Wells have now been vegetarians for more than a year and are happy to report that they are not only healthier but also much slimmer thanks to this change in their diet. They continue to share their experiences with this second volume in their Reluctant Vegetarians series.

Please Review

I hope you have enjoyed this book and will post a favorable review. Independent authors rely on feedback from readers like you to spread the word about books you enjoy. You can leave your comments and contact the author directly by visiting the Geezer Guides web site.

Geezer Guides (the publisher of this book) frequently promotes new titles by offering free copies on special one day only sales. As one of my readers I would like you to get all my new books without charge. Just visit http://ebooks.geezerguides.com and get on their mailing list by filling out the simple form there.

The first volume in this series, available in paperback, audio and electronic formats. Please visit our web site and blog for more information -

http://reluctantvegetarians.com

The third volume in this series, available in paperback, audio and electronic formats. Please visit our web site and blog for more information -

http://reluctantvegetarians.com

Learn how sugar is poisoning you and how the "Evil Empire" has been profiting for hundreds of years.

http://reluctantvegetarians.com

Discover how you can break your sugar addiction and escape the clutches of the :Evil Empire".

http://reluctantvegetarians.com

Made in the USA
Monee, IL
21 February 2023

28428107R00035